EXPERIENCING
the
RESURRECTION

STUDY GUIDE

EXPERIENCING
the
RESURRECTION

STUDY GUIDE

The Everyday Encounter That Changes Your Life

HENRY & MELVIN
BLACKABY

with THOMAS WOMACK

MULTNOMAH
BOOKS

EXPERIENCING THE RESURRECTION STUDY GUIDE
PUBLISHED BY MULTNOMAH BOOKS
12265 Oracle Boulevard, Suite 200
Colorado Springs, Colorado 80921
A division of Random House Inc.

Scripture quotations are taken from the New King James Version ®. Copyright © 1982 by Thomas Nelson Inc. Used by permission. All rights reserved.

Italics in Scripture quotations indicate the authors' added emphasis.

ISBN 978-1-59052-758-0

MULTNOMAH is a trademark of Multnomah Books and is registered in the U.S. Patent and Trademark Office. The colophon is a trademark of Multnomah Books.

Printed in the United States of America
2008—First Edition

10 9 8 7 6 5 4 3 2 1

CONTENTS

ABOUT THIS STUDY GUIDE

What an encouraging word—*resurrection*. It's a word full of hope, a word that inspires and brings courage to those who know Jesus Christ. He's the risen Lord, in whom all authority has been given in heaven and on earth. And those who are in Christ are in a good place.

—*Experiencing the Resurrection*

How do we make the most of this "good place" that is ours in Christ? What does the resurrection of Christ really mean for us? What does it reveal about the heart and mind of God? And what real differences can the miracle of the resurrection make in the lives of believers today?

We'll discover answers to those and other questions as we examine God's Word through this companion study guide to the book *Experiencing the Resurrection* by Henry Blackaby and Melvin Blackaby.

THE SETUP FOR EACH LESSON

At the beginning of each lesson, you'll find a list of the chapters in *Experiencing the Resurrection* that correspond to that lesson. We encourage you to read along in that book as you proceed through this study.

> Throughout this study guide, paragraphs printed in a shaded box (like this one) are excerpts from the book *Experiencing the Resurrection*. These excerpts can help you focus on that book's most important

> themes and conclusions. Read them attentively to center your mind on these key points, even if you've already been through the book.

Each lesson is structured simply, with a series of numbered questions interspersed with quotations from the book. Sometimes a question will be based on the book quote that precedes it. Sometimes the quote that follows the question will amplify the question's purpose and help you reflect on it even more. Many questions also include Scripture references to look up.

The last few numbered questions in each lesson will help you summarize what God has been teaching you and respond to Him by obeying what He is showing you to do.

Each lesson closes with a Scripture passage for meditation and memorization.

The lessons in the last half of this study guide tend to be longer than the earlier lessons. At the beginning of each lesson you'll see a suggestion for how many questions to answer daily in order to complete that lesson in a week or less.

Finally, don't forget that the Holy Spirit is your teacher. Start and end with prayer each time you open this book to work on one of the lessons. Do the same for each group discussion time if you're going through this study with other believers (see the leader's guide at the end of this book).

You can be confident that as you remain open to the Spirit of God, He will change your mind and your heart by the mighty power of the resurrection of Christ.

THE RESURRECTION IN THE HEART AND MIND OF GOD

A companion study to the introduction and
chapters I–2 in *Experiencing the Resurrection*

✦ By answering only three or four questions each day, you can complete this
entire lesson in a week or less.

> Without the resurrection, the cross is meaningless....
>
> The resurrection is proof of Christ's victory over sin and our hope
> of salvation.
>
> The resurrection, however, is not a doctrine to be pondered but an
> invitation to experience the living Christ in your life....
>
> The resurrection power that raised Christ from the dead, then
> seated Him at the right hand of the Father and put Him over all prin-
> cipalities and powers, is the same power given to us. Should that make
> a difference in our lives? Should we be afraid of spiritual warfare? Is
> there anything we cannot overcome if we're walking with Christ?

1. In your understanding, what real difference should the resurrection of
   Jesus Christ be making in your daily life?

> When you become a Christian, you're set in a wholly different dimension in which you can see what others don't see. As Jesus told His disciples, "It has been given to you to know the mysteries of the kingdom of heaven, but to them it has not been given" (Matthew 13:11). **If you've been given ability to understand the mysteries of God, are you using your spiritual senses to detect the activity of God? Or do you act like the world, ignoring God until you need Him to bail you out of a crisis?**

2. For your own life, how would you answer the authors' questions in the preceding quotation?

> You need to know what God is doing and then make whatever adjustment is needed to participate in His redemptive activity.

3. As you continue learning from God in this Bible study, are you committed to making whatever adjustment is necessary in your actions and attitudes as you experience God at work in your life? If so, how would you express that commitment personally to God?

> Unfortunately, many Christians are living way below their potential, believing they'll never be anything but ordinary.

4. In what ways, if any, have you seen yourself as only "ordinary"? In what ways might this have caused you to be living below your potential?

You've been given the opportunity to function in the realm of resurrection power—the most exciting life you could ever imagine. **What then could God do in your life if He knew you were wholly yielded to Him? What could He do in and through you if you believed He has *already* blessed you with every spiritual blessing, delivered you out of the kingdom of darkness, and taken you who were dead in sin and made you fully alive in Christ?**

5. How would you express your answers at this time to the authors' questions in the preceding quotation?

True knowledge of God is always *personal, powerful,* and *life changing....*

The first step in this journey is knowledge. You must *know* the truth and understand what God has done in the resurrection.

Second, you must *believe* it's true for *your* life. The Holy Spirit has been assigned to help you accept the truth as real, by testifying to your spirit that what you're seeing is true.

Third, you must *receive* the truth into your life. It isn't good enough to know the truth or even believe the truth. You must *embrace it as yours.*

> Last, you must *live* the truth. That means taking what you've learned and *acting* upon it—making it a part of your daily life.
>
> Move through this entire process, and you'll find new life in Christ—a life beyond anything you could imagine.

6. Think carefully about the process described by the authors in the preceding quotation. How is this process taking place currently in your life?

> When it comes to the resurrection…it's crucial that we understand *God's* perspective and not try to impose our thoughts upon Him.…
>
> The cross was necessary because of the work of sin in our lives. The resurrection was necessary because the cross put Christ to death on our behalf.…
>
> Our need for these acts of God through the gospel is brought home to us through the reality of our guilty conscience and the conviction of our spiritual deadness.

7. Read through Paul's words in Romans 1:16–28. In your own words, how would you summarize what it says about (a) *how* God reveals His truth to us and (b) *what* is the essence of that truth?

In our passage from Romans 1, Paul said three times, "God also gave them up." What a tragic statement! He let them be enslaved to what they chose over Him. "God gave them up to uncleanness, in the lusts of their hearts" (verse 24); "God gave them up to vile passions" (verse 26); and "God also gave them over to a debased mind, to do those things which are not fitting" (verse 28). Can you think of a more dreadful state than for God to give us over to that which will utterly destroy us in time and for eternity? God gives us up...and steps back.

8. In the world around you and in the lives of people you know, in what ways do you see the tragedy of Romans 1:24–32 being lived out?

The gospel of Jesus Christ is God's clearest revelation of Himself. The incarnation, the crucifixion, the resurrection, and the sending of His Spirit together represent mankind's only hope.

Although God has revealed Himself in many ways, Jesus Christ is the climax of that revelation.

9. How have you seen in your own life that Jesus Christ is truly your "only hope"?

Sin had to be removed before we could move toward our holy God. Sinful humanity cannot come into the presence of a holy God, so the holy God sent His Son, Jesus, to die on the cross to pay the penalty for your sin. He took your sin and died on your behalf.

Whereas the cross put to death your old life, the resurrection brings new life. The old life of sin cannot enter a holy place called heaven; new life in Christ is required. And this new life of resurrection power is made a reality for us through the Holy Spirit.

And here's the most amazing thing about the gospel: the power of the cross and resurrection is just a prayer away. It's that simple. To be simple is not to be shallow or insignificant. To choose Christ is the most profound and substantial decision of your life.

10. Have you truly made the decision to choose Christ? Do you know Him? And are you seeking to know Him more fully?

The gospel story defines us as believers. If you don't understand the cross and resurrection, you don't understand the nature of God or what our faith is all about.

11. How would you define yourself and your own life in terms of the gospel story?

When we talk of the resurrection, we're looking at something more than a stone rolled away, empty burial wraps, and an angel's proclamation.

The cross and resurrection are the heavenly Father's plan to provide salvation for every person who ever walked this earth. It was in His heart from eternity....

His ultimate answer to the question of sin is found in the cross and resurrection, but He'd been working long before then to make us holy.

12. How do the following passages indicate that the cross and the resurrection were part of the Father's plan in eternity past?

Acts 2:22–24

Titus 1:2

1 Peter 1:20–21

Revelation 13:8

How serious is our sin? Serious enough for the Father to ordain His own Son to die a cruel death in our place....

More than all the atrocities of man, the cruel death of Jesus on the cross tells best how serious sin is from God's perspective.

13. Think about Jesus as the sacrifice for your sin. With that truth in mind, what is most important for you to know and understand about Him in each of the following passages?

John 1:4

2 Corinthians 5:21

Hebrews 4:15

Hebrews 7:26

All sin has always been *against* God, and He will not dismiss it lightly.... Our sin profanes His name—and the world is watching.

14. What charge did God make against His people in Ezekiel 36:22?

Ask Him this: "Lord, is there anything in my life that misrepresents You to people who are watching? Has my life become a stumbling block to those who want to know You? Lord, cleanse my life and make me holy before a watching world."

15. Take time to ask the Lord those questions mentioned in the preceding quotation. What are His answers?

> If you ask the heavenly Father to make you holy before a watching world, He'll turn you to the cross and say, "Take a good look. This is My provision for your sin." The Father's plan to remove our sin was the death of Christ; His plan to free us from sin was the resurrection of Christ.
>
> This was His plan from eternity....
>
> In the heart of God, the cross and resurrection were planned before all time, and it was out of His heart that the cross and resurrection came into this world's history.

16. How would you personally summarize the glorious truths mentioned in these passages?

John 3:16

2 Corinthians 5:19

> Do you still think of God only as a harsh judge who condemns? Or have you considered the Father's love for you, that He sent His Son to pay the price for your sin?

17. As you deeply examine your heart, how would you answer the questions raised by the authors in the preceding quotation?

> The Son chose to be obedient unto death.... He left Himself in the hands of the Father with absolute confidence; the promise of the Father would be fulfilled in the resurrection....
>
> Can you see the eternal purpose of the Father in the death and resurrection of the Son?

FOR EXPERIENCING THE RESURRECTION

18. As you conclude this lesson, what has God taught you through your study here? What is the most pressing thing He has brought to your heart's attention?

19. To respond obediently to Him, what must you do at this time?

The Son *had* to die; the Father *had* to raise Him from the dead.

FOR MEDITATION AND MEMORIZATION

That I may know Him and the power of His resurrection, and the fellowship of His sufferings, being con-
formed to His death, if, by any means, I may attain to
the resurrection from the dead.

PHILIPPIANS 3:10–11

THE REALITY OF SIN:
HE DIED

A companion study to chapter 3 in
Experiencing the Resurrection

♦ By answering only two or three questions each day, you can complete this
entire lesson in a week or less.

> The resurrection of Jesus was necessary because of the simple fact that
> He died. So to fully understand the meaning of the resurrection, we
> must first seek to better understand what it means that Jesus died.

1. From His words in John 10:14–15, 17–18, what does Jesus want us
   to understand about the cross and the resurrection?

> *Why did Christ die?* and *What does this have to do with me?* We'll never
> understand resurrection power until we first deal with these questions.

Resurrection power follows death; it's built upon the sacrifice Jesus made on the cross. And though it happened two thousand years ago, it has everything to do with our lives today....

Why did Jesus die?...

The reason Christ had to die was that *sin is real and present in this world,* and *the wages of sin is death.*

2. What is the wonderful promise made about Jesus in the angel's words to Joseph recorded in Matthew 1:21?

It isn't hard to convince people they're sinners, for we all know that we've sinned. We all know our mistakes, our poor choices, our ungodly thoughts, and our selfish desires. What we don't grasp is how truly offensive that sin is to God or how to be free from that sin in order to live lives pleasing to God.

3. Look at Romans 5:6. Why are human beings described this way in this verse? And why is it important for us to view humanity in this way?

We can't grow in appreciating the resurrection without a deeper grasp of what it means that Christ died for the ungodly.

4. What has Christ done about this ungodliness, and how should we respond, according to Titus 2:11–15?

Our own hope of resurrection is not just a future event that occurs when we physically die and are transported into heaven; its impact is meant for today. When the Bible speaks of resurrection, especially as it applies to our own lives, it's almost always in reference to the power to overcome the sin that's within us. But in heaven there is no sin. So our foremost benefit of resurrection power is not for when we get to heaven, but to help us here on earth.

5. Have you tended to think of the resurrection more as something to be experienced in the eternal future or as something you should be experiencing now? Which view has been the strongest in your understanding?

Jesus died for the sin of the world and was raised to conquer sin's destructive power. And all who have been resurrected with Him are no longer under the dominion of sin and death. They are now alive to God and are no longer slaves to sin, but walk in newness of life.

Resurrection power is to free us from sin today and forevermore!

This is why we cannot fully realize the power of the resurrection until we've understood what Christ was resurrected *from*—the death grip of sin....

> For on that cross, sin was dealt with once and for all, while the res-
> urrection was the final stripping of sin's death grip, a blow that echoed
> throughout eternity.

6. How do you think the warning Paul gives in 2 Corinthians 11:3
   applies to your life at this time?

> When it comes to the cross and the resurrection of Christ, Satan will
> try to keep your focus on a body that was beaten, whipped, pierced,
> and crucified. He doesn't mind you thinking about the agony of
> intense pain, the public humiliation, and the innocent blood that
> Christ shed. He isn't bothered if you see the truth of the crucifixion—
> as long as you don't notice *the truth of His death....*
>
> When Christ died for us, it wasn't because we were human, but
> because we were sinners.

7. How are the concepts of "death" and "sleep" referred to in these passages, and what do they teach us about the meaning of death?

Mark 5:23

Mark 5:35–39

John 11:4, 11, 14

To bring back to life those who were physically dead was no great challenge for Jesus. He would simply speak, and they would arise. He almost casually refers to their condition as "sleep" because He had the ability to awake them, giving life by the command of His voice.

Jesus reserved the word *death* to express an experience infinitely more significant. And to fully appreciate the *life* Christ has given us, we need to better understand the *death* from which He saved us. To better understand the magnitude of resurrection power, we must see more clearly what happened at the cross and the nature of Christ's death.

So before we look further at resurrection life, we must see that contrast.

8. What do these passages teach us about the death of Christ?

Romans 5:6–8

1 Corinthians 15:3

Galatians 2:21

On the cross, [Christ] experienced more than just the cessation of physical life. He died in the eternal sense of the word....

At Calvary, as Jesus hung on the cross, He made this statement: "My God, My God, why have You forsaken me?" (Matthew 27:46). That was true *death*—even before the termination of His physical life.... He'd already entered a place He'd never entered before.

Jesus had never sinned; He was the perfect Son of God. But

because the sin of the world was placed upon Him, and the wages of sin is death, the Son's relationship with the Father was struck a death-blow. For the first time in His eternal existence, He was in spiritual darkness. The sight of the Father's house was now obscured. The Father's hand was withdrawn.

Jesus was in utter darkness. He was suffering the agonizing loneliness of sin that separates humans from a holy God. For that homelessness of the soul—that separation from the heavenlies into outer darkness—is the wages of sin.

9. What is the inescapable result of sin, according to Romans 6:23?

When we explore resurrection life and its power to transform, we need to rearrange our thinking into a whole new dimension that goes beyond the physical into the realm of the spiritual, where our souls dwell....

There's a dimension to the resurrection that we experience the moment we believe in Jesus. This is sometimes referred to with the phrase "already, but not yet." Believers already experience the power of the resurrection, though they'll experience it in a fuller way when Christ returns.

10. What do we learn about both life and death from Romans 8:1–2?

The good news is almost unbelievable: no matter how deep and ugly our sin, Christ's sacrifice is much greater....

The only thing now keeping us from a relationship with God is our will, refusing to believe and accept God's provision for us in Christ. That barrier is overcome when we choose to step out in faith and receive Him.

This is not an elusive doctrine; it's a reality to live out in daily life....

From Jesus' perspective, **spiritual life is reality and physical life can distract us, pull us away, and keep us from seeing what will last for eternity.**

So we must take His words by faith and move beyond those physical distractions. We must make the choice to believe what Christ has said and to live in the reality of the risen Lord. And then we come to experience how the resurrection in its essence is freedom from sin.

11. In your life, what are the distractions that most often tend to keep you from maintaining an eternal perspective about your existence and purpose in life?

FOR EXPERIENCING THE RESURRECTION

12. As you conclude this lesson, what has God taught you through your study here? What is the most pressing thing He has brought to your heart's attention?

13. To respond obediently to Him, what must you do at this time?

FOR MEDITATION AND MEMORIZATION

He made Him who knew no sin to be sin for us, that
we might become the righteousness of God in Him.

2 CORINTHIANS 5:21

THE REALITY OF SALVATION: HE ROSE

A companion study to chapter 4 in
Experiencing the Resurrection

✦ By answering only two or three questions each day, you can complete this entire lesson in a week or less.

> People have always been haunted by the thought of death. But now that Christ has been resurrected, there's no need to fear death anymore. Death has lost its sting; we can escape everlasting punishment for sin and, with it, eternal separation from God.
>
> Physical death is now but a transition into our new and glorious existence in God's presence; it's the shedding of our weak and frail bodies and the receiving of new resurrection bodies. That is, *if* we choose to accept the gift of salvation, to repent of our sin, and to make Christ the Lord of our lives.

1. To what extent in your life have you experienced the fear of death?

> Our resurrection life hinges on the fact that Jesus really did rise from the dead to new life. And if that fact isn't established, our faith is in vain.
>
> So *did* Jesus rise? Did He truly die and then come back to life? This is a valid question that must be addressed.

2. What key truths do these passages indicate about the reality of the physical suffering and death Jesus endured?

    Matthew 26:67–68

    Matthew 27:26, 28–30

    Mark 14:65

    John 19:17–18

> The word *excruciating*—which literally means "out of the cross"—is a fitting description of the ordeal of crucifixion.

3. How do these passages indicate that Jesus did indeed die?

    Matthew 27:57–60

    Luke 23:46

John 19:30

John 19:34

> People who don't want to believe that Jesus is the Son of God will con-
> jecture anything to try to disprove His death and resurrection.... Jesus
> was crucified...and He *died* on the cross.

4. How did the authorities ensure that the lifeless body of Jesus would
   remain in His grave, according to Matthew 27:62–66?

> The enemies of Jesus ensured that Jesus would stay in the tomb and
> that nobody was going to take away the body.
>   They did a good job; *nobody* stole Jesus' body from the tomb.
>   Jesus died and was buried, yet three days later His tomb was
> empty. Not many argue this point. Everyone recognizes that *something*
> happened to the body.

5. Look at the specific confirmations of Jesus' resurrection in each of
   these passages. What importance do you see for each one?

Matthew 28:5–7

Matthew 28:8–10

Luke 24:15–16, 28–31

Luke 24:36–43

John 20:11–18

John 20:19–21

John 20:26–29

John 21:1–14

Acts 1:3–11

1 Corinthians 15:5–7

So the resurrection was confirmed not only by physical evidence but also by divine messengers.

> It was also confirmed by many personal appearances of the risen
> Lord—the most convincing evidence of all. The disciples saw Jesus
> alive for themselves....
>
> Jesus was seen in many places, by many people, on many different
> occasions. This had to be real and no illusion.

6. After the resurrection and ascension of Jesus, how would you describe
   the character and attitudes displayed by His Spirit-filled disciples
   (especially Peter), as seen in these passages early in Acts?

   2:14, 32, 36, 38–40

   2:43

   3:2–7

   3:12–16

   4:8–14

   4:18–20

   4:31

4:32–33

> Perhaps the greatest change caused by the resurrection was in the character of the disciples. They had previously been timid, afraid, and depressed after witnessing the arrest and suffering of Jesus. But after His resurrection they became aggressive, bold, and full of joy.…
>
> When you observe the post-resurrection disciples, you see that they had *life!* Their circumstances didn't matter. They had joy in the midst of suffering and peace in the midst of turmoil. Nothing could take away their passion arising from the everlasting life they'd received from Christ.

7. Look again at Peter's words in his Pentecost sermon in Acts 2:22–36. As he explains the resurrection of Christ, what is most important in what he says?

> Peter's words [in Acts 2:22–36] present the first apostolic statement on the resurrection. Peter was declaring with absolute certainty, "God raised up Jesus—the man you nailed to a cross."
>
> Remember that Peter was speaking to a crowd in Jerusalem, the city where Jesus died. Many in that crowd had probably been eyewitnesses to Jesus' crucifixion, which had happened there less than two months earlier. His execution had been a prominent event in the city, one that no doubt was a topic of discussion for a long time. Peter was talking to people keenly interested in what he was talking about.

> In Peter's words to them, the resurrection was just as much a fact of history as the crucifixion—a fact with immediate and powerful results. And the reason Peter gave for the resurrection is simply this: it wasn't possible that Jesus could be held by death.
>
> The world today says, "It's impossible for Jesus to rise from the dead." But Peter said, "It's impossible for Jesus *not* to rise from the dead."

8. Peter quotes Psalm 16 in this sermon. Look up this psalm. How does it point to Christ's resurrection—and to ours?

> Christ's resurrection was foretold not only by Old Testament prophets, but by the Lord Himself…: "Jesus began to show to His disciples that He must go to Jerusalem, and suffer many things from the elders and chief priests and scribes, and be killed, and be raised the third day" (Matthew 16:21). Divine prophecy is a guarantee that death couldn't hold Jesus in the grave.

9. Look up Acts 3:14. On this later occasion, as Peter again addresses a crowd in Jerusalem, what title does he use as he refers to Jesus?

> Peter was convinced that *life* was the nature of Jesus....
>
> Jesus *is* life; He is self-existent over and above that which we call death. He lives forever because He *is* life and has become the source of life for all who believe in Him.

10. What do these passages from the gospel of John indicate about Christ as the essence of life?

   1:4

   5:26–29

   11:25–26

   14:6

> Resurrection to new life is not just a physical transaction. There's a spiritual transaction that takes place, giving new life to the believer. And the power that raised Christ from the dead is the exact same power *we* experience as we walk in Christ, the giver of eternal life....
>
> That is the essence of salvation—new life in Christ Jesus.

FOR EXPERIENCING THE RESURRECTION

11. As you conclude this lesson, what has God taught you through your
    study here? What is the most pressing thing He has brought to your
    heart's attention?

12. To respond obediently to Him, what must you do at this time?

FOR MEDITATION AND MEMORIZATION

The last enemy that will be destroyed is death.

1 CORINTHIANS 15:26

THE REALITY OF ETERNITY: HE IS ALIVE

A companion study to chapter 5 in
Experiencing the Resurrection

✦ By answering only two or three questions each day, you can complete this
entire lesson in a week or less.

> Tragically, many people here rarely think of eternity, much less prepare
> for it. Nevertheless, whether or not we're prepared, all human beings
> will face it and will realize the consequences of their preparation.

1. What particular uniqueness of Jesus is emphasized in 1 Timothy 2:5?

> Why is Jesus the only one through whom we can go to heaven?
> Because of *the resurrection*.
>   The resurrection of Jesus is unique among all religions in the
> world. Every religious leader who has ever walked this earth has died

> and is still dead to this day. Jesus alone has been resurrected from the
> dead—not resuscitated back to life, but resurrected into new life.

2. Jesus appears to the apostle John in Revelation 1. As we think about
   the resurrection, what is the significance of the way Jesus describes
   Himself to John in verses 1:17–18?

> Jesus came *from eternity.* He stepped into time and space and lived on
> this earth to communicate the truth about eternal life and to provide
> our safe passage into it. His perspective on life and death is much dif-
> ferent than ours—and He's telling the truth....
>
> The most important thing about Christ's death and resurrection
> was not physical but spiritual.... He was physically dead, and He was
> spiritually dead. For the wages of sin is *death*—spiritual separation
> from the heavenly Father.
>
> Once the price for sin was paid in full through the death of Christ,
> the heavenly Father raised Him from the dead—physically and spiritu-
> ally. It was not resuscitation, but resurrection. He conquered sin and
> death, and His resurrection is proof positive.

3. How would you characterize "eternal life" from the words Jesus spoke
   to Martha in John 11:25–26?

His resurrection demonstrated that beyond physical death is a place more wonderful than we can imagine, in the presence of God.

When Jesus said we would have abundant life, He was talking about *eternal life*. Because He lives, we too shall live. Resurrection is a state in which believers *enjoy* their eternal destiny—a life beyond this life.

The resurrection is the clearest evidence that eternity is real and that everything must be seen against the backdrop of eternity.... Eternity was His focus. Living forever was what the resurrection accomplished.

4. Look at how Jesus is described in Hebrews 5:9. How is this significant in helping you see your life "against the backdrop of eternity"?

5. How is Jesus' understanding of eternity—as it relates to *our* eternal future—conveyed to us in His words in Matthew 25:31–46?

The promised power of the resurrection applies only to those who obey Him. Eternity awaits everybody, but new life is only for those who obey.

6. What reality about evil is revealed to us in Ephesians 6:12, and why is this important for us to understand?

7. What important truth about God is stated in 1 John 1:5, and how does this relate to our eternal future?

> So many people...don't understand their own condition against the backdrop of eternity....
>
> How far is it between light and dark? They aren't even in the same room. If there's any light there at all, then it isn't dark. Likewise, to live in the state of sin means that you're completely removed from the God of light—and desperately in need of a Savior.
>
> Eternity is real, hence the need for resurrection. Jesus therefore is the key to eternal life. He's the One who died for our sins and then rose victorious over sin and death....
>
> He's "alive forevermore" (Revelation 1:18)—what a wonderful statement!

8. After His disciples experienced success in ministry, what strong reminder does Jesus give them in Luke 10:17–20?

Don't be distracted by success. Don't find your joy in accomplishments. Don't find your identity in the things you do or the job you have.

Instead, rejoice in this and this alone: *your names are written in heaven!* Rejoice in the fact that God has chosen you, that God has blessed you, that God is working through you. Your great joy is found in your relationship to God, who has made a way for you to enjoy eternity with Him. And through your life, He's working to bring others to eternal life through the gospel of Jesus Christ.

We should never get distracted by good works or a successful ministry, but simply be thankful for our salvation. We should be endlessly grateful that we're saved from sin and born into the family of God, especially with the knowledge of what it cost to provide eternal life.

9. What does it truly mean to you that your name is written in heaven?

Being a Christian…means a relationship with the risen Lord. It means living the new life He provided through the resurrection. That reality impacts every area of our life. It sets new priorities and submits the temporal to the eternal.

Resurrection changes everything. It changes the way we raise our children, for now we realize that their souls are eternal. It changes the way we invest our money, for all material things will be burned up, and only that which is eternal will last. It changes the way we use our time, for time on earth is short, while eternity is forever. It changes the way we see people, for no matter how evil they may appear, we don't want to see anybody sent to eternal judgment.

10. What areas of your life need to be more impacted by the truth of the resurrection—by your relationship with the risen Lord?

> The primary concern of Jesus was to secure our souls for eternal life.
> **What is the priority of your life?**

11. How would you answer the preceding question from the authors?

FOR EXPERIENCING THE RESURRECTION

12. As you conclude this lesson, what has God taught you through your study here? What is the most pressing thing He has brought to your heart's attention?

13. To respond obediently to Him, what must you do at this time?

FOR MEDITATION AND MEMORIZATION

Do not be afraid; I am the First and the Last. I am
He who lives, and was dead, and behold, I am alive for-
evermore. Amen. And I have the keys of Hades and of
Death.

REVELATION 1:17–18

RESURRECTION LIFE

A companion study to chapters 6–7 in
Experiencing the Resurrection

✦ By answering five or six questions each day, you can complete this entire
lesson in a week or less.

> The cross and the resurrection began in the heart of God. They were
> lived out in the life of Jesus Christ, God's Son.
>
> But their full impact hits *our* lives: *we* are the reason the Father
> sent His Son. The cross and resurrection were not for the sake of Jesus,
> but for our sakes.
>
> And as a result of what the Father has done, the resurrection is
> something believers can experience in daily life…as well as something
> we'll experience for all eternity.

1. Review again the account of the resurrection in Matthew 28:1–8.
   What two instances of "fear" are recorded here—and how are they
   different?

Just as the women responded to the resurrection with "fear and great joy," so we are overwhelmed at its prospects. New life always brings great joy, but the power of the resurrection also instills a sense of fear. We realize very quickly that this is outside our scope of experience. It's not something we control; rather, it controls us. The divine has interacted with the mortal. Eternity has crossed into time.

We have no prior reference point for the resurrection. It's uniquely a divine act of God....

This resurrection power was not of this world; it was beyond the scope of any earthly experience. The world demonstrates power by taking life, but God demonstrates His power by giving it.

2. Think carefully about Paul's familiar words about the living Christ in Galatians 2:20. How would you explain in your own words what Paul is saying here?

Somehow, in Paul's life, he lingered long enough at the foot of the cross that he began to experience within himself the pain and agony that Christ felt. Christ had endured this pain and agony on Paul's behalf, and Paul internalized this experience. And as a result, he would never again be the same....

He understood the depths of what sin had done to the Lord, and in his spirit, Paul went to the cross and died with Him. He took the time at the cross to understand that event very intimately—so much so that he could say, "I have been crucified with Christ; it is no longer I who live, but Christ lives in me."

> In our lives, there must also come a point when we can truly say, "I have been crucified with Christ."

3. How do Paul's words in Galatians 2:20 relate to the instruction Jesus gave His disciples in Matthew 16:24–26?

> This resurrection power is available to all human beings—with only one condition: *you must die.* The power of the resurrection is found in the ability to die. Resurrection power is on the other side of a conscious decision to die to self and give your life to Christ. It requires a decision of the will to be crucified with Christ, that the Father might raise you to new life....
>
> Let us say it again: the secret to resurrection power is that you must die before you can be resurrected.

4. In Philippians 2:8–9, what is the connecting point between the death of Christ and His being exalted (in His resurrection and ascension) by the Father?

5. In regard to this truth about Jesus, how are we commanded to respond in Philippians 2:5?

Think back to Jesus' life. Did He resurrect Himself? No, the Father raised Him up. What part did Jesus play? *He died.* He obeyed the Father unto death.

Likewise, the power of the resurrection is what the Father does in you when you die to self and choose to live in Christ. *You die; the Father resurrects.*

He does not resurrect you to a better life, but to a new life.

6. What resurrection truths about us are stated in Ephesians 2:4–6, and why are they significant to you personally?

Physically, we're born and live until we die; *we progress toward physical death.* Spiritually, we're dead until we're made alive in Christ; *we progress toward eternal life.*

So the kingdom of God is exactly the opposite of the kingdom of the world.

7. What resurrection truths about us are given in Romans 6:4–5, and why are they significant to you personally?

Jesus is alive—and we can trust Him to lead us to eternity with His Father. The resurrection is proof that He knows what He's talking about.

Recall again that when the Bible speaks of resurrection as applied to our lives, it's nearly always talking about the power for overcoming sin. There's so much more to the resurrection than going to heaven when you die. In fact, the power of the resurrection is primarily strength for today. It gives victory over sin and tears down the wall separating us from God. It frees us from the dominion of darkness and brings us into the kingdom of light. It provides a relationship with the risen Christ, who loves us and gave His life for us. It's what opens the door to all God has promised to those who put their trust in Him....

Death and resurrection go together; dying to self and living with Christ cannot be separated.

8. Review Paul's words in Philippians 3:7–10. For Paul, what was the personal significance of Christ's death and resurrection as stated here?

Resurrection power is something you can *know;* newness of life is something you can *experience*—if you so choose....

So let us ask you three simple questions. First, **do you *want* resurrection life? Do you really want to know the power of the resurrection and the life God created you to know?**

9. What is your honest response to the above question from the authors?

We're convinced that most people do *not* want [resurrection life]. They want to go to heaven when they die, but they don't want His power on earth. For with the power comes responsibility; with the power comes accountability. There's an expectation that you have to act godly—and who wants that? There's the obligation to live like Jesus—not just in His resurrection but in His cross.

10. What expectations do you have that go along with wanting resurrection life?

Our second question is this: **Are you *pursuing* resurrection life? If you say you want resurrection life, does your life demonstrate that desire? Would others conclude that you want to know Christ and the power of His resurrection because of how much time you spend in prayer? and in His Word? and with His people? and in worship? From watching the way you live your life, would others conclude that you want to know the Lord more than anything in the world?**

11. What are your honest responses to the above question from the authors?

Would we know you're walking with Christ by how you make decisions in life, because you've been reoriented to eternal priorities? Do you consult Him when you make your plans? Have you chosen to give Him first place in your schedule?

12. Again, what are your honest responses to these questions from the authors?

Would we know that Christ is your all in all by your conversations? Do you love to hear stories of what He's doing in other people's lives? Do you ask others what He's doing? Do you share with others what He's doing in you?

13. And again, what are your honest responses to these questions from the authors?

Third question: **What is your *decision*? Will you give your life completely to Christ, that you might know the power of the resurrection and the fellowship of His sufferings?**

14. What is your decision?

> If there's a hesitation to answer that question, don't expect to experience Him in your life. For He is not yet Lord. You may want Him to be Lord, but you aren't willing to go to the cross and die.

15. As we come to worship and hear God's voice, what are we warned about in Psalm 95:7–8?

> Deep down in your soul, **do you hear the call of God wanting more of you?**

16. How would you answer the above question from the authors?

17. Look at what Jesus says about Himself in Luke 4:18–19 (quoting from Isaiah 61). How do these callings upon His life from the Father find fulfillment in Jesus' resurrection, especially as we share in it with Him?

> The Lord says, "Stop eying the reward—keep your eyes on Me. It is not just heaven someday; it is life today. Make a choice to receive Me...all of Me. Take My life, death, and resurrection."

> **What will it look like for you to live in the power of the resurrection? Can you say right now that you are experiencing new life in Christ as God intended? Do you believe you're expressing that power adequately to your family, your church, and the world?**
>
> If not, you need to die to self and allow Him to live in you. It's a choice!

18. For your own life, how would you respond to the questions from the authors in the preceding quotation?

> The characters in the Bible were ordinary people—faced with extraordinary situations. They had to choose to walk by faith or to walk by sight. Those who chose to walk by faith experienced the mighty power of God working in their lives. They got to live an uncommon life with an extraordinary God.
>
> If you want to live in such a way as to experience the resurrection, you'll find yourself in the middle of impossible situations. The resurrection itself is impossible—it's in the realm of the divine and beyond anything you can do in your own strength. It is God-sized in nature. As you experience it, don't be surprised if God takes you into things that are impossible for the average human being. Resurrection life brings uncommon experiences and takes you where you never would have gone otherwise. And it challenges your faith to its furthest limit.

19. To what degree are you expecting and asking God to take you into "impossible" situations?

If you're asking God to let you experience the resurrection, you're asking Him to take you into a place you've never been. So don't complain when He does.

God never does things the way we think they should be done. His ways are not our ways; His thoughts are not our thoughts. That's why faith is required to follow Him. Faith is fundamental to the resurrection life as God leads us into impossible situations. He takes us to the end of ourselves—and beyond.

It has always been that way....

Resurrection life is about walking with God. Every time a person moves into that arena of divine life, miracles happen. This is true in the Old Testament, in the New Testament, and today.

---

20. Read Exodus 14:10–31, and examine the situation Moses found himself in. What aspects of "the uncommon life" did he experience here?

21. Read Joshua 6:1–21, and examine the situation Joshua found himself in. What aspects of "the uncommon life" did he experience here?

22. Read Judges 7:1–22, and examine the situation Gideon found himself in. What aspects of "the uncommon life" did he experience here?

> Time after time, God took people into impossible situations and then displayed His power in their midst. *That's how God works.*

23. In Matthew 14:22–27, look carefully at the situation the disciples found themselves in. What specific danger were the disciples in?

> Jesus put them into danger—and didn't even go with them! Well, that's only half true. Jesus did come to them a bit later—*walking on the water.*

24. Look closely at Matthew 14:28–30. What appears to be particularly true about Peter in this moment as he responded the way he did?

> Remember, Peter wasn't alone in that boat. All the other disciples were right there watching this scene unfold before them. But they

remained in the boat while Peter was out with Jesus walking on the waves. He may have been a little crazy, but you have to admire his courage.

25. How would you describe the response Jesus gave to Peter in Matthew 14:31?

Peter still had a ways to go, but he was growing in faith right before his Lord's eyes. Everyone else was still in the boat, but Peter was living life on the edge. He was learning more each day about the uncommon life of a disciple.

Have you been in that place? that place where Jesus takes you, the place of no return?

26. What is your personal response to the above question from the authors?

Don't always assume that a difficult situation is a result of some mistake you made. Perhaps God brought you to this difficult situation so you might see His mighty power....

Be assured: *you're in a good place.* You may be where God has been leading you all along. He had to get you where you are now so He can show you more of Himself than you've ever known.

> So don't quit. Don't hesitate. Don't turn back. Simply call out His name. Depend on Him! For He has you right where He wants you.

27. What patterns do you see in the way that you typically respond to difficult situations?

> When it comes to God, His way *is* the "high" way. He moves on a plane much higher than we do. He doesn't function within our limitations. He isn't restricted by nature's laws; He made nature. He is God!
>
> And following His ways, with Him in full control, is resurrection life at its best.

28. In what ways might you need to yield more completely to God's full control of your life?

> One of the ways God teaches you to trust Him is to place you in a church that's walking by faith. It's a great place to be, walking together with other believers who are following after Christ. We can pray for one another, encourage one another, walk with one another, and give one another strength when we face the impossible.

29. How are you experiencing the resurrection life—the uncommon life—in your church at this time?

Why did Jesus have Peter come to Him on the water? So Peter could brag to his friends? No, it was because He was shaping the character of Peter to be a great leader in the early church. The early Christians would need a spiritual leader who knew Christ and would walk by faith. Peter would prove to be such a man, full of faith and confident in Christ....

So why does Jesus ask *us* to step out in faith and walk to Him? Is it so we can tell other people of all our accomplishments? No, He's building our faith to prepare us for greater assignments that await us within the kingdom of God—things that will require an absolute confidence in God to do the impossible.

30. How is God shaping your own character at this time? How are you responding to the "impossible" situations He's bringing into your life?

Are you one who has looked back with longing eyes to the great stories of the Bible and wished you could have been there?... Today is *our* day to see the mighty power of God. This is *our* day to walk with the resurrected Jesus. This is the life available to all who would believe.

> These are great days to walk with Jesus and see the mighty power of God in our midst. We'll look back upon these days and marvel. But it will take faith; it will take courage.

31. Do you have the faith and courage to trust God to display His mighty power in the circumstances of your life and your church life at this time?

> Only the Lord knows what He wants to do in your life. So ask Him.
>
> Perhaps the Lord is telling you to get out of your comfortable boat. But you're scared. *Trust Him.*
>
> Perhaps you're personally going through a storm. *Keep your eyes on Jesus.*
>
> Perhaps your confidence in God was strong, but now you're distracted and overcome with doubt. *Refocus on Him.*
>
> Impossible situations are normal in the Christian life. This is how God builds our character and brings glory to Himself. The way of resurrection life is an adventurous road. Let's take it!

32. Write here your prayer response to the Lord at this time:

> As you progress in this resurrection life, it not only leads you into an exciting walk with the Lord, it changes you deep inside. It begins to

produce in you a Christlike character. You become a living example of
the power of the resurrection to bring new life to that which is dead.

FOR EXPERIENCING THE RESURRECTION

33. As you conclude this lesson, what has God taught you through your
study here? What is the most pressing thing He has brought to your
heart's attention?

34. To respond obediently to Him, what must you do at this time?

FOR MEDITATION AND MEMORIZATION

> Peter answered Him and said, "Lord, if it is You, com-
> mand me to come to You on the water." So He said,
> "Come."
>
> MATTHEW 14:28–29

RESURRECTION PEACE AND JOY

A companion study to chapters 8–9 in
Experiencing the Resurrection

✦ By answering only three or four questions each day, you can complete this entire lesson in a week or less.

> You can always tell those who are walking in a right relationship with Jesus. They're at peace. They're content.
>   Could anything feel better than to know you're at peace with God?

1. How do these passages indicate that we have been in "a state of war" with God? And how has God responded to our hostility?

Romans 5:9–10

Colossians 1:21–22

Titus 3:3–5

Before you knew Christ, you were at war with God and in rebellion against the King of kings. But now there is peace. Your soul is no longer struggling; you are right with God. Your status has changed....

The underlying meaning of the biblical word *peace* has to do with relationship. It's "harmony of relationship" or "reconciliation between two parties."

2. In these verses, how does Jesus emphasize the peace that comes through a right relationship with God?

Luke 7:50

Luke 8:48

John 14:27

John 16:33

John 20:19, 21, 26

He says to you and me, "Peace I leave with you."

He wants you to be at peace, so why do so many lack peace in their hearts? Why is it that so many are anxious, worried, stressed, restless, and on edge?

> It's because we all want peace, but few are willing to do what's necessary to obtain it....
>
> Nobody can expect to know the peace *of* God if they're not at peace *with* God.

3. On the hills outside Bethlehem, when the angel appeared and told the terrified shepherds, "Do not be afraid" (Luke 2:10), what was the basis and reason for that encouragement to them?

> If we were to stand before a holy God as people who remain in sin, we ought to be very afraid. God's Word says that the wages of sin is death, so to continue to live in sin is to lose life forever.
>
> So how does God bring peace? He offers forgiveness of sin and a restored relationship. Jesus is the Prince of Peace, but you will know peace only if you make Him Lord of your life....
>
> Jesus brings peace, but to experience it, you must come to Him on His terms. Are you walking in a relationship with Christ that brings peace? It's a choice.

4. What vital aspects of this peace are revealed to us in Romans 5:1–11?

Peace with God—through a relationship with Christ—will introduce us to the grace of God. The peace of Christ brings us into the sphere of God's grace in which we stand before Him.

5. Look at what Jesus prayed in John 17:13. What does He want His followers to experience?

Why was the Lord so concerned that they be full of joy? Because He knew that the message they would preach would mean nothing if they weren't full of joy. If the resurrection did not make a qualitative difference in their lives, why would anyone want to hear the gospel? But He knew that a joyful life and the corresponding countenance on their faces would convince people of the reality of freedom from sin and hope in Christ.

Jesus also knew that there would be many difficult days ahead for the disciples, and the world would watch to see how they would respond to those difficulties.

The disciples would prove that a relationship with God brings joy, and everything else pales in comparison to a relationship with the risen Christ.

6. How do we see the joy of Christ's followers in these passages from Acts?

5:42

13:52

20:24

7. Look also in the following pages at what the apostles taught the early church about joy. What was significant about their teachings on joy?

Philippians 4:4

James 1:2

1 Peter 1:8

1 Peter 4:13

1 John 1:4

If you've lost the joy of the Lord, you've lost sight of the resurrected Lord. I'm not talking about losing your salvation, but losing the *joy* of your salvation. If you've lost the joy of serving the Lord, you're in trouble! It's an indication that you've moved away from Him, that you're no longer filled with His Spirit.

The sense of joy that comes from an encounter with the risen Lord grows only deeper as you walk with Him. Once you come to know peace with God, joy springs forth like an ever-flowing well.

The Christian life is not just an emotion. But how can you receive forgiveness for every sin you've ever committed, experience absolute peace with a holy God, have assurance of salvation and a home in heaven, know victory over temptations to sin, and walk in fellowship with Jesus Christ—yet not have joy?

The resurrection life is one characterized by joy. It can be no other way.

8. How deeply are you currently experiencing the joy of your salvation?

9. How is joy realistic or even possible in a world so filled with tragedy, cruelty, and disappointment?

Abiding joy is clear evidence that you have peace with God and are experiencing a deep relationship with the living Christ. A person walking with the Lord is a realist. He or she understands the seriousness of life and the reality of spiritual warfare, but that doesn't rob that person of joy....

Yes, the Christian life requires dealing with eternally serious issues in life, but Christ is the answer to those issues, and that's what brings such joy; it's what produces abundant life in Christ.

10. How then would you define true joy?

Humor and laughter are both wonderful and necessary parts of experiencing life to its fullest. A great story can change the atmosphere of a room, filling it with laughter. *But this is not the joy of the Lord.* We can know the joy of entering a beautiful church building and singing wonderful songs of worship, getting caught up in an emotional lift through stirring and powerful music. *But this is not the joy of the Lord.* There's joy that comes simply from being with believers you've come to love and cherish. *But this is not the joy of the Lord.* There's joy from reading comforting words from Scripture, hearing truth from God's Word that touches the soul. *But this is not the joy of the Lord.*

None of these things are *opposed* to resurrection joy. They are, however, poor substitutes for what we're talking about.... The deepest expression of resurrection joy can come only from the resurrected Christ. It's a by-product of the love relationship you have with Him....

For sure, a genuine relationship with Christ *will* produce Christian fellowship, heartfelt singing, the study of His Word, and intimate times of prayer. But never let these activities be a substitute for the relationship. Jesus is not a doctrine to believe in; He has been resurrected, and He offers a real and personal relationship to all who come to Him.

11. What source of joy does Jesus reveal to us in John 15:5, 9–11? How would you express this in your own words?

12. In a typical day in your life, how much of it is spent experiencing true joy?

There are times when the Lord is probably telling us, "Lighten up! Don't be so uptight all the time! Why so downcast? Why so sad? Why do you act like serving Me is so terrible?"...

If joy is present deep down in your heart, it cannot be hidden. It will eventually show up on your face.... It ought to be expressed in the words you say, the tone of your voice, and the look in your eyes. It ought to be known in the way you sing. Joy will find its way into your relationships, both with intimate friends and with strangers. People ought to look forward to your greeting, for they know that you'll encourage their lives with a joyful encounter.

13. Look at the truth stated in each of the following passages. How can each one serve as a reason for joy?

Romans 8:28

Philippians 1:21

Philippians 3:20–21

> When you realize that joy is the fruit of a relationship, not of an activity, then you have the ability to rejoice in the Lord always. For you're experiencing the perfect fulfillment of that for which God created you.

FOR EXPERIENCING THE RESURRECTION

14. As you conclude this lesson, what has God taught you through your study here? What is the most pressing thing He has brought to your heart's attention?

15. To respond obediently to Him, what must you do at this time?

FOR MEDITATION AND MEMORIZATION

> Therefore, having been justified by faith, we have peace
> with God through our Lord Jesus Christ, through
> whom also we have access by faith into this grace in
> which we stand, and rejoice in hope of the glory of God.
> ROMANS 5:1–2

RESURRECTION POWER
AND AUTHORITY

A companion study to chapters 10–11 in
Experiencing the Resurrection

♦ By answering five or six questions each day, you can complete this entire
lesson in a week or less.

> Dynamite demolishes, breaks apart, and can even take life. But the
> gospel of Christ does exactly the opposite of dynamite. Paul is ex-
> pressing how the power of the gospel brings wholeness and gives new
> life.
>
> Which has more power—that which takes life or that which gives
> life? The greatest power on earth is to give life to that which is dead,
> and God alone holds such power.

1. What does God reveal to us about power in Romans 1:16?

> *Life* is the essential nature of resurrection power....
>
> Resurrection power always has to do with *life*. And God has placed this exact same power within every believer. He intends to bring life through those who have come to experience abundant life in Christ.

2. What promise of power did the resurrected Lord Jesus make to His followers in Acts 1:8, and how does it relate to their own experience of the resurrection?

3. What is the essence of the New Testament's teaching on power as given in these passages?

   1 Corinthians 1:18

   1 Corinthians 2:4–5

   1 Corinthians 4:20

   2 Corinthians 4:7

   Ephesians 3:20

Over and over we're told of a power given to believers in Jesus. But do we experience it? Are we living in that power? Or have we become satisfied with giving God our best, missing out on a power given to us the moment we believed in the resurrected Lord?

4. Look at Paul's prayer in Ephesians 1:19–23. What do these words reveal about the resurrection power that is ours to experience?

The power that raised Jesus from the dead and gave Him authority over all things is the same power *we* should experience as believers. This power that defeated sin was to be experienced not in heaven but on earth. This power that broke the rule of Satan was for the purpose of freeing people in this world from his authority. This power is to be realized in us and through *us*.

His power, *His* strength, *His* might, *His* authority is to permeate the church. For Christ has been made head of the church, and we are His body. The church is both the object of His blessing and the instrument through which He touches the world.

5. What would you say is the greatest demonstration of God's power in the world today?

His greatest power is displayed not in the natural realm, but in that which is supernatural and impacts eternity. While God may choose to bring back physical health and restore a diseased or injured human body, the greatest miracle of God is what He does to the soul that is dead. He has the power to give eternal life—He revives the spirit within us by breathing new life into us, lifting us to a place much higher than ever imagined. He brings us to Himself, and we live in the presence of the holy. And in that place, we experience the divine (2 Peter 1:4)....

God's greatest miracles are found in the human soul....

We'll know we're in the center of God's will and living according to His purpose when we see His power working in us and through us to bring transformation to people and entire communities.

6. What outworking of God's power is taught in the words of Jesus in John 8:34–36?

7. What demonstration of God's power do we see in Acts 4:31–33?

The early church consisted of plain men and women who were both insignificant and unknown. It began with no equipment or resources like we enjoy today. It fought against fierce persecution and hatred, yet they had the power to turn the world upside down (Acts 17:6). Perse-

cution fell upon these early Christians with a fury, yet they emerged
stronger and more powerful than any movement the world had known.

Such power was the realized impact of the resurrection. Victory
was already won, and the early believers claimed it as their own in the
name of Jesus.

8. Read about what Jesus said and did in Luke 5:18–26. From what this
incident reveals, how would you compare the power required for
physical healing with the power needed to accomplish forgiveness of
sin?

According to Jesus, it takes far more power to forgive sins than it does
to heal the physically infirm. From an earthly perspective, He had the
power to heal the man of paralysis and give him a higher quality of life.
From an eternal perspective, He did a far greater miracle. He forgave
the man's sin and cleansed his soul.

Physical healing required not power but a casual word. Forgiving
sin, however, required an all-encompassing and life-giving expression of
power. The cross and resurrection represent such a powerful moment in
time that both the physical and spiritual world shook.

What if Jesus, when He came to earth, had healed the lame, the
lepers, and the blind, yet never conquered sin in the cross and resurrection? Those He ministered to would have experienced longer and
healthier lives, but they would still have died and gone into eternity
with no hope. We too would have had no benefit from His time on
earth.

Fortunately, Jesus was not distracted from the priority of eternity. Resurrection power primarily has to do with eternal life. This is true for Jesus, and it should be true for us.

9. In your own understanding, what does it mean personally for you that resurrection power primarily has to do with eternal life?

As a believer in Jesus Christ, you have the power to give the gift of eternal life. Not because of who you are, but because the resurrected Jesus dwells within every Christian. *He* has conquered sin and death and is ready to share His victory through your life. But Satan will do everything possible to keep you from that truth. He wants to keep your focus on the physical world and leave the spiritual world a mystery that's left for a future experience in heaven. He wants us to keep truth locked in our heads—and distant from everyday reality.

10. In what ways has the spiritual world been kept too much of a mystery for you, instead of an everyday reality?

You can always tell when someone hasn't experienced the resurrection. They're still working hard in their own power to serve God. They haven't learned to let the risen Christ live through their life. Instead, they do their best to help people. It isn't that they don't care, or even that they don't love others. The problem is that they still think the resurrection is something they'll experience only when they die and need a new body for their days in heaven. So they work hard in their own strength because they believe that's all the strength they possess. Oh, they may believe "theologically" that they're a "new creation" in Christ, but they have no idea what this means in daily life. As a result, the world gets the best *we* have to offer and misses out on the best *God* has to offer.

11. What has Christ's resurrection meant for you personally in providing strength for ministry to others?

True love cannot look the other way when there's the capacity to help someone in a destitute or unhealthy condition. But God's love cannot stay there—it must go further. It must meet people's ultimate need, whether they're aware of their spiritual need or not.

12. In John 8:24, what did Jesus say about those who remain in their sin? And what does this reveal about people's ultimate need?

So [Jesus] died in our place and went to the grave—but with the full confidence that the power of the Father was sufficient. And indeed, the Father went after Him and reached down into the darkness and laid hold of His Son. With all the power of Satan and his demons straining

> to secure the grave, the righteous right hand of the Father found its
> way. And the power of almighty God ripped His Son from the eternal
> chains meant for you and me. The resurrection power pulled Him
> from a pit of darkness back into the kingdom of light.

13. What does Colossians 1:13–18 reveal to us about the wonder of resurrection power?

14. How do you see resurrection power relating to the essential truths of the Christian life that are taught in these passages?

   2 Corinthians 3:18

   2 Corinthians 4:7

   2 Corinthians 4:16

   2 Corinthians 5:20

> Now that Christ lives in us, He is our identity. We're in the process of
> being conformed to His image. We're ambassadors of Christ, and as
> such, we carry His authority. And with His authority comes His power
> to give life.

15. What fundamental truths do we learn about the dynamics of spiritual power and authority in each of these passages?

Matthew 28:18–20

Luke 10:17–19

Ephesians 1:22–23

Colossians 2:9–10

As Jesus spoke to His disciples for the last time on earth, He said this: "All authority has been given to Me" (Matthew 28:18)....

And what's most amazing about this is that His authority over all things is expressed through the lives of believers....

Remember, *all* authority has been given to Jesus. And in some way, He has transferred that authority to believers; He has given to us the keys of the kingdom of heaven.

16. What dynamics of spiritual power and authority does Jesus teach to His disciples in Matthew 16:18–19?

Jesus was saying to the disciples, "You will be a part of letting people into the kingdom. You won't just say empty words. Rather, the power of the living God that's at work in your lives will work through you to help others as well."

This would be the strategy of God for all time. Through the lives of transformed people, He would bring salvation to the world. The power of the resurrection that brought life to them would spread through them to those who would encounter their lives.

Do you understand that you've been given the keys of the kingdom? You've been given the "key words" of the gospel that sets people free from sin. The kingdom will come as we receive these keys from the Lord and *use them*. As we go into the world under His authority and share the gospel story, the Spirit of God will take those words and convince the world of truth.

17. As you think about the "keys of the kingdom of heaven" and the power and authority they represent, what opposite force does Jesus expose in Matthew 23:13, 27?

We're partners with God. We're co-laborers with Him. We've been given the keys to life!

So we must ask ourselves some serious questions: **Are we using the keys Christ has given us? Are we going out to share the gospel? Are we living in a manner worthy of the gospel?**

18. How would you answer the bolded questions above?

If you think about your life and the impact it's making on the world, is there any evidence that you've received the keys of the kingdom of heaven?

19. Again, how would you answer this question from the authors?

How you use the keys of the kingdom will either let people in or keep them out....

If we leave the keys on the key rack at home, we're closing the doors of heaven to those who are bound by sin....

We can lock the doors to heaven for others in several ways. First, we keep people out by refusing to speak of Jesus....

Second, we keep people out of heaven by being a stumbling block—when the way we live our lives as Christians becomes a deterrent for people....

Third, we keep people out of the kingdom of heaven through disobedience to the Lord. We choose to remain comfortable with our lifestyle and refuse to follow the Lord as He goes to set people free....

There are many ways we can be a hindrance to the work of God, and we'll all be held accountable for how we've responded to His call.

20. Are there any ways in which you have been locking out others from the doors to heaven?

So how do you do it? How do you experience the power of the resurrection that unlocks the door to the kingdom of heaven?

It's only through a deep and abiding relationship with the resurrected Christ. **Do you have that kind of relationship?**

21. To what extent can you describe your relationship with the resurrected Christ as "deep and abiding"?

You can experience the power of the resurrection through your relationship with Christ, but you must do three basic things to experience it.

The first step is *repentance*.... You cannot remain in sin and experience the power of the resurrection. It's spiritually impossible. You must repent of your sin and ask forgiveness so that your sin may be removed....

If you want resurrection power, you must be cleansed of your sin.

22. How have you followed this step of repentance? In what ways is further repentance required?

Is there any sin in your life that's hindering your relationship with Christ?... Is there any questionable habit or behavior in your life? Get rid of it; run from it; don't let anything weigh you down.

23. What is your response to the bolded question from the authors on the previous page?

Is there any bitterness or ill will toward another? Be reconciled with that person, and seek to live in peace with everyone.

24. Again, what is your response to this question?

Is there still a tendency toward pride and selfish dreams? Put it away, and ask the Lord to give you a humble and contrite spirit.

25. Again, what is your response?

Second, *obey completely* what the Lord is asking of you....

Is there anything that you know God wants you to do that you haven't done? Immediately obey. **Are there promises you've made to God that you haven't kept?** Do what you've promised; make it right. In God's eyes, delayed obedience is disobedience. Do the last thing He told you, and remain in His love.

26. What is your response to these questions from the authors on the previous page?

The third step is to *seek the Lord with all your heart.* Don't be satisfied with past glory, but seek after Him with renewed fervor. **Is there a longing to know Him more, or are you content to stay in the comfort zone? How long has it been since you've been refreshed by the presence of God?**

Go to Him, run to Him, and search for Him with all your heart. Your relationship with Christ is the key to knowing resurrection power.

27. Again, what is your response to these questions from the authors?

28. Look once more at what Jesus tells us in Luke 9:23. What is God showing you about pride and selfishness in your life?

Self is the greatest hindrance in life. Our human nature seeks to rob God of His glory and take it for ourselves. Our natural life is affected by sin—and pride is a thief. Our pride will keep us from ever knowing

God's power in our lives, for God will not share His glory with just anyone; He will not use those who can't handle it....

You are your own worst enemy! The fact that you're trying to please the Lord by working hard is a sign that you're rebelling against the finished work of Christ on the cross and are neglecting the power of the resurrection.

29. In what ways have you recognized that you are your own worst enemy?

30. Look at Acts 4:13. As people encountered the boldness of Peter and John, what did they realize about them?

Do people recognize that we've been with Jesus and He has completely transformed our lives? Do they hear endless words from us about Jesus? Do they sense that we truly know Him?...

What is it about your life that makes you different?

31. In your own life, how would you answer these questions from the authors?

The world doesn't need to see how good we are, but to see the perfect Son of God in our lives. So is there a recognizable difference in our lives that begs the question, "By what power have you done this?"

FOR EXPERIENCING THE RESURRECTION

32. As you conclude this lesson, what has God taught you through your study here? What is the most pressing thing He has brought to your heart's attention?

33. To respond obediently to Him, what must you do at this time?

FOR MEDITATION AND MEMORIZATION

And with great power the apostles gave witness to the resurrection of the Lord Jesus. And great grace was upon them all.

ACTS 4:33

RESURRECTION
CONFIDENCE AND HOPE

A companion study to chapters 12–13 in
Experiencing the Resurrection

✦ By answering four or five questions each day, you can complete this entire
lesson in a week or less.

> Anyone who has an intimate relationship with Jesus Christ is a person
> who lives a life of ease. That does not mean life is easy for them but
> that life is not complicated or stressful. They live with a childlike faith
> that's absolutely confident in God's love.
>
> "If God is *for* us" (Romans 8:31), then why is there any reason to
> fear? We don't need to worry about what the future holds, for the hand
> of God is leading us into the future.

1. Review the parable Jesus told in Matthew 7:24–27. What was the
   same about both of these houses?

> Every last one of us will endure trouble. Sooner or later, it will come. And when it comes, where do you turn? From where do you gain your strength? Have you learned to stand with the risen Lord and enjoy His power to overcome?

2. What is your response to the above questions from the authors?

> There *is* trouble in the world—that's a given. And to endure it, we must go to the One who has overcome it.

3. What does Jesus promise us in John 16:33?

> In times of suffering, some want to ask, "Why did this terrible thing happen to me?" But we should be asking, "Why does God love me? Why does He forgive me when I sin? Why does He forgive me when I fall into that same sin again? Why does He continue to seek me when I forsake Him? Why does the holy God love a sinful person like me? How could this wonderful thing happen to me?"...
>
> In light of God's love, God's mercy, God's grace—trials and tribulations look much different. As we stand with the risen Lord, the world just seems to take on a new look....
>
> Our greatest problem is that we fail to recognize there's a positive

and redemptive purpose to every problem we face. Until we confront this reality, we'll be helpless victims of problems all through our lives.

4. In your own life, how have you benefited from going through trials and hardships?

So why do trials come?
- *Because we're human and live in a fallen world.* Disasters, troubles, and illness are common on earth.
- *Because we sin or disobey God.* Our bad choices bring undesirable consequences.
- *Because God wants to discipline us.* Parents understand that love means discipline, correction, and training for our children. In the same manner, God uses our trials to instruct and train us in how to walk with Him.
- *Because hard times lead us to the Bible.* They drive us to search God's Word for answers. Trials push us to reestablish priorities and seek truth to guide our lives.
- *Because in moments of crisis, our fellowship with God moves to a deeper level.* Difficulties heighten our dependence upon Him and help us realize that nearness to God is for our good.
- *Because trials teach us to pray with fervency.* Too often we neglect prayer until we encounter suffering.
- And sometimes trials come *because of reasons we don't know.* There are times God allows trouble, and it doesn't make any sense. But we must choose to trust Him anyway.

5. What have you learned about trusting God as a result of the trials and hardships you've experienced?

In the midst of suffering, we're drawn closer to the Lord than perhaps at any other time in our lives. This isn't true of everyone.... But to those who trust in God and have learned to walk with Christ, something miraculous happens in their lives through suffering.

6. List some of the hardships Paul experienced, named in 2 Corinthians 11:23–27. How do these compare with your own trials?

When the Lord is with you, you can proceed with confidence, knowing that He sees you, that He understands the big picture, and that He is aware of all the details in your life. You can rest assured that He has the power to do whatever He desires; miracles are His specialty. He has a purpose for allowing trials into your life, and His actions toward you come from a heart of pure love.

You don't have to fear or let anxiety overcome you; the risen Lord is with you. You never have to say, "Poor me," in His presence. Instead, you'll find yourself saying, "How fortunate I am to have a God who loves me, a God who will never leave me nor forsake me. And how wonderful it will be to someday shed this mortal body and live with Him eternally!"

7. Look at the promise in Psalm 91:1. How can this be of help in our trials?

We've discovered that it's not just tribulation that upsets our lives; God Himself can turn our world upside down. When God begins to work in mighty power, our lives are unsettled. And only those who are prepared will stand. Only those who are strengthened with His might will be able to endure His activity. God tests our faith through trials to see if we're ready for His mighty work. Just as steel is tested to ensure that it can handle the load of a great bridge, so our faith is tested to see if we can handle the mighty work of God before it comes. When our faith is sure, God pours out His Spirit in power among us.

Just walk with the Lord and you'll be ready for tribulation; you'll be ready for God's Spirit to come in power. And you'll be ready for whatever comes to your life. And by your response, the world will see God. Even more important, *you* will see God living out His purpose in you.

8. What are the strongest ways that you've seen God Himself upsetting your life—turning your world upside down?

The confidence we know in Christ is found in our new relationship with Him: we're family....

> *You belong.* You're in the family of God. God has no orphans. You belong in His household.
>
> Can there be anything that gives us more confidence in life than to walk with Christ in the family of God?

9. According to 1 John 3:1, what does God's love accomplish for us?

> John moves beyond speaking about love as being "shown" or "revealed" or "manifested" to us by God to describing how He *bestowed* His love *upon* us. He has put His love *into* us—infused or injected His love within us.
>
> The key word in this verse is *that*—or properly, *in order that*. God bestowed His love upon us for this purpose: that we might become children of God....
>
> That's why the Bible talks so much about Christians loving others. God's love flowing out of us is the evidence that we have God's nature within us—and therefore the proof that we've been born again.

10. What fundamental truth about God's love are we reminded of in Romans 5:5?

> Those who have known the presence of the Lord will be souls at rest. They're not anxious or worried about tomorrow; they confidently live day by day in the presence of the Lord. And their lives are making a

difference. The power of the resurrection to bring life leaves a trail of transformation wherever they go. By the time their lives on earth are drawing to a close, there's confident expectation of eternity with Christ. Their countenance is full of grace, and the tender spirit of the Lord consumes them. They're a joy to be around; they uplift everyone who knows them. They're living in the joy of their salvation, and they know the presence of Christ.

But those who haven't met the Lord will grow increasingly restless. In their older years, they tend to be known as people whose name starts with *G* and ends with *rumpy,* causing others to keep their distance. They've become frustrated at their inability to make a lasting difference, they become anxious as the end draws near, and they feel helpless to do anything about it.

11. In 1 Corinthians 15:12–58, Paul says much about the resurrection of Christ and about our own resurrection. Read over the concluding portion of this passage, in verses 50–58. What important encouragement for all believers is found there?

One of the most important implications of resurrection is that if we're in relationship with Christ, we no longer have to fear death.

12. What have been your main expectations about what you'll encounter in eternity?

> There's a good chance that when we first glimpse heaven, it will be like nothing we could have imagined.

13. What does 1 Corinthians 2:9 reveal about how God prepares things that we cannot anticipate? And who are these surprises specifically for?

> We cannot talk about experiencing the resurrection without talking about the hope we have in Christ—the hope of a better place after our physical bodies pass away....
>
> The greatest mystery in the world is that God desires the resurrected Christ to dwell in the hearts of those who believe and to be their "hope of glory."

14. What does Colossians 1:26–27 teach us about our "hope of glory"?

> Biblical hope is not like the world's hope. To the world, hope is wishful thinking. But when our hope is in God, we have confident expectation that He'll do everything He has promised. Hope in God has no doubt; it is not questioned. For believers in Christ, hope is reality waiting to be experienced.

15. When Jesus uses the word *heaven* in Matthew 6:9, what does He mean by it?

Heaven is a place beyond human experience. It's the source of everything good. It's the object of our hope. It's the future home of those
who have put their faith in Christ.

16. Summarize what Revelation 21:4 says about the future for Christians.

Heaven is a place where all negative things are absent. We'll enjoy freedom from the things that weigh us down here on earth.

17. What are you most looking forward to in heaven?

Heaven, however, is not just the absence of things which cause us sor-
row. It's also the presence of everything that brings true joy.

18. What do these passages teach us about our eternal future?

Matthew 5:8

Matthew 8:11

Matthew 16:27

Romans 8:35–39

1 Corinthians 13:12

Philippians 1:21–24

1 John 3:2

Revelation 14:13

What a hope! Paul's concept of eternity is rooted in the hope of resurrection—of being in the presence of the resurrected Lord Jesus....

In heaven, we'll experience perfect love—and there's nothing a person wants more. There's no more loneliness in heaven, but only pure love beyond description. We'll be enveloped in God's loving arms, and we'll remain in His loving embrace for eternity....

Heaven is also a place of fellowship. We'll enjoy the blessing of friends old and new....

Heaven also is described as a place of rest....

Heaven is a place of great reward....

Above all, heaven is a place where we'll see the Lord face to face.... Oh, to enjoy the presence of the Lord! What can we say? It's one thing to look into the heavens and see His handiwork. It's another to look straight into His face and see His love.

As this study concludes, examine your life once more as you consider carefully the following review questions from the authors, and record your responses to each one.

> Are you truly *living*, in the eternal sense of the word? Do you know the forgiveness of sin through Jesus Christ, and are you living free from its grip on your life? Death is separation from God; life is abiding in His presence. Can you say you're in His presence right now, without anything hindering that relationship? If not, then bring the power of the resurrection to bear upon your life by asking Christ to come and cleanse you of all sin. In prayer, repent of your sin and ask Him to bring you into the presence of almighty God.

19. Your response:

> Are you experiencing an uncommon life? Are you living in such a way that people see Christ in you, doing that which you could not do on your own? If not, why not? Don't act like a mere mortal; live the life God has given you as a child of God. You partake in the divine nature and have the capacity for so much more than the world around you. Don't limit yourself by your abilities, but allow the resurrected Christ to live through you in power. Die to self, and allow Christ complete lordship of your life. This life is not about what you can do for God, but what He can do through you. In prayer, tell the Lord that your life is His to use. You want your life to bring glory to Him.

20. Your response:

Are you experiencing resurrection peace? You don't have to live with guilt and shame, but can experience a soul at peace with God. Every time Satan reminds you of your past, just remind him of his future. Christ has won the victory, and you're free! If your past seems to be haunting you, holding you back from moving forward, stop and pray. Ask the resurrected Lord to fill you with His peace. Ask Him to confirm in your spirit that you are completely forgiven and in right standing with God.

21. Your response:

Are you full of the joy of the Lord? Jesus expressly stated on many occasions that His resurrection brings great joy. Even in the midst of trials, you can have joy that cannot be taken away. It means that circumstances don't control your heart, but the Spirit of the Lord does. So if you've slipped into depression and have lost the joy of your salvation, stop and pray. Ask the Lord to do what He promised—to fill you with His joy. Ask Him to cause His joy to burst forth into visible expression, that others might be drawn to Christ, who is alive in you.

22. Your response:

Are you living with resurrection power? The power that raised Jesus from the dead is the exact same power that's at work in your life. Those areas of your life that have been dead are now alive. Your spirit has been awakened, and you now have the capacity to know God in His fullness. That power is at work to bring abundant life.

So if you sense there must be more to the Christian life than you're experiencing…there probably is. And it's to be found only in a relationship to Christ. Ask Him to open your spiritual eyes to see all that He has prepared for you. Linger in His presence as long as it takes to become fully aware of His life in your life.

23. Your response:

Are you living under the authority of Christ? Is your life worthy of the gospel? The life you've received is to be shared with those around

> you who are still dead in trespasses and sins. Christ has given you the keys of the kingdom of heaven. He has entrusted you with the greatest power on earth—the power of the gospel. Share it freely, live it fully, and share the power of the resurrection with all people. We'll be held accountable for what we've done with the gospel, so ask the Lord to use your life to bring others into the kingdom. Don't watch from a distance, but get in the game. Pray for the Lord to give you an opportunity to be a part of His great plan of salvation.

24. Your response:

> **Are you standing strong, confident in your walk with God and grounded in Christ? Or are you easily shaken by circumstances?** Stability, faithfulness, and confidence are marks of one who's walking with Christ. Ask God to show you what you have trusted in for life's stability. It could be your job, your family, your health, or your talents. None of those can compare to trusting wholeheartedly in Christ. If you're aware of things that have replaced Christ as the foundation of your life, ask Him to forgive you. Ask Him to rebuild your life.

25. Your response:

Are you living in the hope of your salvation, or are you afraid of death? There should be no fear of eternity in the heart of a believer, but confident expectation that everything God has promised is *yes* in Christ. When that's true—when eternity is secured in your heart—the petty things in life cannot weigh you down. The little things are irrelevant compared to an eternal reward in heaven that's everlasting in nature.

26. Your response:

FOR MEDITATION AND MEMORIZATION

For if we have been united together in the likeness of
His death, certainly we also shall be in the likeness of
His resurrection.

ROMANS 6:5

LEADER'S GUIDE

♦ These introductory remarks are adapted from the *Experiencing the Cross Study Guide* by Henry Blackaby with Brian Smith.

As you join with others to learn more about Christ's resurrection and our part in it, remember that the Scriptures are your trustworthy guide—not only the passages listed in this study guide, but also other passages the Lord will lead you to as you're open to His guidance.

Remember too that the Holy Spirit Himself is your faithful teacher. You can be confident that He will lead you into truth, by the power of the Lord's promise: "When He, the Spirit of truth, has come, He will guide you into all truth" (John 16:13). Be assured that God's Spirit wants to reveal to all of you Himself and His ways. He will instruct you through the Scriptures and also through each person in your group.

As God does this, He will require adjustments from each of you. Obediently following through with these adjustments is the key to experiencing God's great salvation in your life.

As the group's leader, spend time considering how these principles should influence the way your group functions.

SOME GROUND RULES

When you first get together, consider asking the group members to agree to the following guidelines to help everyone get the most out of this group study experience.

- Talk about making a commitment to be learners *together* and to be encouraging supporters of one another along the way. This study on experiencing Christ's resurrection calls for revolutionary life change. But many people will be willing to take such daring steps of growth only in a setting where they feel safe. Make a group commitment to lovingly accept each other.
- Encourage each group member to do his or her best to complete all the questions in each week's lesson.
- Encourage everyone in the group to read through *Experiencing the Resurrection* by Henry Blackaby and Melvin Blackaby. The corresponding chapters in that book are listed at the beginning of each lesson. This will involve reading one or two chapters for each lesson.

YOUR PREPARATION

As the group's leader, pray diligently about your responsibilities and for all the group members by name. Pray for the Holy Spirit to speak to all of you during your personal study time as well as during your discussion time together.

For all the participants, ask for supernatural blessings from the Holy Spirit and for spiritual insight into eternal truths.

Ask for personal discoveries and breakthroughs where these are most needed in your lives.

Ask for protection from disunity, selfishness, and pride; ask for growth together in unity, servanthood, and humility.

As you study and prepare each week, consider writing out in this guide's page margins the text for several key Scripture passages the group will be looking at. This is a good exercise in becoming more familiar with the passages, and it will also mean that the text for them will be immediately at hand during your discussion time.

Review all the questions in each week's lesson, and decide ahead of time which ones you think are the most important to discuss.

GROUP DISCUSSION

Remember to include prayer as you begin your group discussion—not a token "Bless our time together," but a sincere request for the Holy Spirit to guide your discussion and your learning of the Father's will and purposes. Expect God's Spirit to be in control.

At some point in each week's session, allow for a time of group prayer when all the members are free to communicate with the Lord about the things you're learning together.

In the discussion, take the lead in sharing honestly from your own life. This will help encourage the others to do so as well. Talk about what you're learning, or still trying to learn, about the lesson. Keep the discussion focused on God's commands and purposes and on your personal application of them.

Here are week-by-week suggestions for life-changing discussions:

LESSON 1—THE RESURRECTION IN THE HEART AND MIND OF GOD

You may want to begin by spending plenty of time discussing everyone's expectations of what they want to learn from this study.

Question 1: Encourage everyone to articulate what they seek and how they want their lives to change as a result of better understanding the resurrection of Christ.

Question 2: The questions allow for a simple yes or no answer, but encourage everyone to reveal the reasons for their answer and to explain them more fully.

Question 3: As you share together these commitment statements, take a moment to pray together and express these commitments to God.

Question 4: Getting beyond these low expectations and assumptions will be a key purpose that is evident throughout this study guide.

Question 5: Spend plenty of time opening your hearts and minds to all that's possible in our lives when we truly believe and experience God's promises.

Question 6: Spend enough time here to ensure that everyone clearly understands this life-changing process.

Question 7: You may want to read this passage aloud before you discuss it.

Question 8: After discussing the answers to this question, you may want to ask something like this: "How does God want us to respond to this tragic situation we see all around us?"

Question 9: Though Christ is truly our only hope, we all have tendencies to look elsewhere for it. Where else do we look?

Question 10: Establish whether each person in the group has indeed made this decision to choose Christ.

Question 11: You may want to make sure everyone truly understands the essentials of the gospel.

Question 12: Help everyone get a glimpse of the Father's love, wisdom, and sovereignty in planning from eternity past for our salvation through Christ.

Question 13: After discussing these passages, you may want to spend time together in prayer, praising the Lord Jesus for being the perfect sacrifice for our salvation.

Question 14: Help everyone see that our response to sin and to the gospel is more than just a private and personal affair.

Question 15: You may want to focus here again on prayer together.

Question 16: The purpose here is to help everyone view the gospel in a fresh way—as we always should!

Question 17: Help everyone search their minds and hearts to fully realize how they honestly view God.

Question 18: Spend plenty of time here, and encourage each person to be deliberate and earnest in identifying how the Lord is speaking to them through His Word and His Spirit.

Question 19: Help everyone to be clear and intentional in identifying and responding to what God is asking them to do.

LESSON 2—THE REALITY OF SIN: JESUS DIED

Question 1: Notice in these passages how the Lord Jesus fully yielded to the Father's plan and fully utilized the authority given Him by the Father.

Question 2: Help the group fully appreciate how the Father's plan of salvation was always central to the whole reason He sent His Son to earth.

Question 3: What does "ungodly" mean?

Question 4: What does this say about the Father's character?

Question 5: You may want to remind the group that throughout this study guide, we'll be looking at both the everyday implications as well as the eternal implications of the resurrection of Christ. Both are inseparably linked.

Question 6: Be aware of our constant tendency to move away from a clear focus on Christ and a simple devotion to Him.

Question 7: This distinction about the different understandings of "death" can be difficult to grasp. Make sure everyone understands it.

Question 8: Realize the full weight of the fact that Jesus *died* for us.

Question 9: This point—that sin leads to death—is one that our sinful hearts can easily want to minimize.

Question 10: Help the group appreciate the amazing scope and fullness of our salvation—that it truly is a matter of life and death.

Question 11: It's important to recognize these distractions for what they really are. So often they're "good" things rather than blatantly evil things.

Question 12: Spend plenty of time here, and encourage each person to be deliberate and earnest in identifying how the Lord is speaking to them through His Word and His Spirit.

Question 13: Help everyone to be clear and intentional in identifying and responding to what God is asking them to do.

LESSON 3—THE REALITY OF SALVATION:
JESUS ROSE

Question 1: Sometimes the fear of death has been suppressed or hidden in our lives.

Question 2: Notice how matter-of-fact the Scriptures are in describing the suffering and death of Jesus.

Question 3: Notice again the objectivity and dignity of how the Scriptures describe these details.

Question 4: You may want to remind the group of how many people who have doubted the reality of the resurrection of Jesus have been thoroughly convinced after examining the evidence, even when they wanted to disprove the resurrection. See, for example, the book *Who Moved the Stone?* by Frank Morison.

Question 5: Help everyone see that the Scriptures leave no doubt that Jesus did indeed rise from the dead.

Question 6: Contrast what you see here with how the disciples acted previously, especially in the immediate hours after Jesus was arrested.

Question 7: Spend plenty of time here examining Peter's words in this very first evangelistic outreach in the church's history.

Question 8: Looking at this psalm in light of the New Testament will help us to see the continuity of the Father's plan and the unity of the Scriptures.

Question 9: Explore the significance of this title for Jesus.

Question 10: How do we understand "life"? What does this word truly mean in the Scriptures?

Question 11: Spend plenty of time here, and encourage each person to be deliberate and earnest in identifying how the Lord is speaking to them through His Word and His Spirit.

Question 12: Help everyone to be clear and intentional in identifying and responding to what God is asking them to do.

LESSON 4—THE REALITY OF ETERNITY: JESUS IS ALIVE

Question 1: Work together to keep seeing the uniqueness of Jesus as our way of salvation.

Question 2: Notice from this passage in Revelation that Jesus wants our understanding of these truths to alleviate our fear.

Question 3: Most of us tend to see "life" in a much more limited and ordinary way than how Jesus wants us to understand and experience it.

Question 4: You may want to explore together the question of why God wants us to clearly understand our salvation as "*eternal* salvation."

Question 5: Notice the unbreakable connection between what we do in this life and what happens to us in eternity.

Question 6: What limits us in daily life from being more aware of the realities of our spiritual conflict with evil?

Question 7: Notice the stark "black and white" distinction between God's light and evil's darkness—and fully appreciate the implications this has for all of our life, here and in eternity.

Question 8: Why do we need this reminder from Jesus?

Question 9: Encourage the group's gratitude to God for salvation, and spend time together in prayer expressing it.

Questions 10–12: Spend plenty of time here, and encourage each person to be deliberate and earnest in identifying how the Lord is speaking to them through His Word and His Spirit.

Question 13: Help everyone to be clear and intentional in identifying and responding to what God is asking them to do.

LESSON 5—RESURRECTION LIFE

Question 1: In what ways were these two instances of fear alike?

Question 2: Spend plenty of time here, exploring how we can get to the point of also being able to say what Paul said in Galatians 2:20.

Questions 3–5: Realize together how critically important this understanding of the connection between death and resurrection is.

Question 6: Explore together and fully appreciate how God reveals to us His mercy and grace.

Question 7: What does this "newness" truly represent for us?

Question 8: What specific choices must we make so that we can become able to say the same things that Paul says in this passage?

Questions 9–10: There may be ways in which we are still resisting the experience of resurrection life. Be honest in probing for these.

Questions 11–14: Although these questions allow for simple yes or no answers, encourage the group to use them to find practical, specific ways to seek a more obedient life in Christ.

Questions 15–16: What does it mean to "harden our hearts," as the psalm warns about? Why does it tend to happen particularly when we hear God's voice?

Question 17: How can we have a part in fulfilling these words of Jesus?

Question 18: We return here to the basic reasons for doing this study together. What difference will it make?

Questions 19–22: Each person will have at least one area in which God is wanting them to step out in faith into the unknown, into a greater challenge. Encourage each other to take these steps of risk and obedience.

Questions 23–26: Many times, the need for stepping out in faith is prompted by the "storms" that come into our lives. If some in your group are encountering those storms right now, join with them in facing these things, and encourage them to see each challenge from the Lord's perspective.

Question 27: Be expectant that God's power can help each of you overcome wrong and inadequate patterns in how you typically respond to hardships and challenges.

Questions 28–33: Spend plenty of time on these personal life-centered questions, and encourage each person to be deliberate and earnest in identifying how the Lord is speaking to them through His Word and His Spirit.

Question 34: Help everyone to be clear and intentional in identifying and responding to what God is asking them to do.

LESSON 6—RESURRECTION PEACE AND JOY

Question 1: Many of us often resist the idea of thinking we were ever "at war" with God. This usually comes from an inadequate view of how great an offense our sin is to a holy God, and it tends to diminish our appreciation of the gospel. Help everyone in the group move beyond these limitations.

Question 2: Something else to consider: how did Jesus demonstrate the experience of peace in His own life on earth?

Question 3: The focus here is on recognizing that our deliverance from sin and from the judgment we deserve is our only hope for true peace with God and peace throughout our lives.

Question 4: Notice the connections in this passage between our experience of peace and the facts of the gospel.

Question 5: How is joy related to peace in our experience?

Questions 6–7: Something else to explore: why does joy receive such emphasis in the New Testament?

Question 8: What causes us to lose our experience of the joy of our salvation?

Question 9: Be aware also that the more we fail to see Christ as the answer to all our questions and issues, the more our joy will be diminished.

Questions 10–12: The point here is to see that the kind of joy Christ makes available to us goes far beyond what most of us think of as "joy."

Question 13: Recognize that the grace of God is so abundant in providing for our needs—and above and beyond them—that we truly have every reason for joy and thankfulness.

Question 14: Spend plenty of time here, and encourage each person to be deliberate and earnest in identifying how the Lord is speaking to them through His Word and His Spirit.

Question 15: Help everyone to be clear and intentional in identifying and responding to what God is asking them to do.

Lesson 7—Resurrection Power and Authority

Questions 1–4: In looking at all these passages, strive to gain an appreciation for the kind of power that is meant to be our everyday experience in the Christian life.

Questions 5–8: The point here is to see the continuing miraculous power at work as God delivers people from sin and they respond in repentance and faith.

Questions 9–11: Be aware of the ways we try to compensate when the experience of Christ's power is lacking from our lives.

Questions 12–13: Once again, focus on humanity's fundamental need to overcome slavery to sin.

Question 14: Recognize how clearly the New Testament teaches that our lives are to be characterized by power—and the boldness and confidence that flow from this power.

Question 15: Spiritual power relates closely to spiritual authority. And God intends for us to experience both. What marks the presence of spiritual power and authority in our lives? And what is true about our lives when that power and authority is missing?

Questions 16–20: These questions on the "keys of the kingdom" point us to vital truths. Be aware together of the supreme privilege and honor we have in being granted this authority—as well as the immense responsibility and accountability.

Question 21: Keep coming back to the importance of this vital, abiding relationship with Christ in everything we do.

Questions 22–27: Here are more questions that allow for simple yes or no answers. Once again, encourage the group to use them to find practical, specific ways to seek a more obedient life in Christ.

Questions 28–29: Recognize together how pride and selfishness are at the root of what holds us back from experiencing the uncommon resurrection life of peace, joy, power, and authority. Recognize that pride and selfishness are deeply ingrained and must be constantly recognized and overcome.

Questions 30–31: Help everyone in your group to be excited and encouraged that our lives really *can* make a difference—they really *can* bring glory to God as they draw people to Jesus Christ.

Question 32: Spend plenty of time here, and encourage each person to be deliberate and earnest in identifying how the Lord is speaking to them through His Word and His Spirit.

Question 33: Help everyone to be clear and intentional in identifying and responding to what God is asking them to do.

LESSON 8—RESURRECTION CONFIDENCE AND HOPE

Questions 1–2: Sometimes we think we're entitled to a life that's free from hardship; or at least we think such a life is possible, whether or not we're entitled to it. Why is this a wrong and harmful way of thinking?

Question 3: Focus on Jesus as the One to always turn to in times of trouble.

Questions 4–7: You may want to spend time in prayer together, expressing gratitude to God for the specific blessings He has brought into your lives through particular hardships and trials.

Question 8: Why is it so important for us to recognize God's role in allowing trials in our lives and being in control over them?

Questions 9–10: Why is the experience of God's love so important for us in experiencing true confidence in our lives?

Question 11: As we allow the truth of the resurrection to build up our confidence in Christ, how should that confidence be expressed and lived out?

Questions 12–18: Many of us have very limited expectations of our eternal life in heaven, and sometimes our expectations are misguided and ill informed. Use these questions to clarify in your thinking the fundamental truths of eternity that Scripture makes clear.

Questions 19–26: Spend plenty of time here, and encourage each person to be deliberate and earnest in identifying how the Lord is speaking to them through His Word and His Spirit. Help everyone to be clear and intentional in identifying and responding to what God is asking them to do.

DARE TO GO THERE

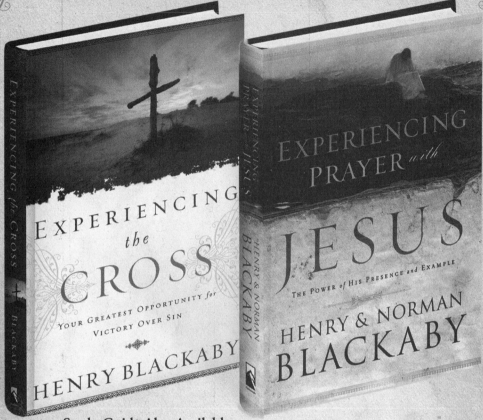

Study Guide Also Available

Experience new depths in your spiritual growth with more titles from the Blackaby family. In *Experiencing the Cross,* Henry Blackaby leads you on an exploration through deeper dimensions of the cross, ensuring that the further you go, the more you will deal radically and completely with sin. *Experiencing Prayer with Jesus* will help you discover freedom from methods and formulas, the beauty of a gentle step-by-step reformation process and let God unfold his mighty purposes for you.

Available in bookstores and from your favorite online retailers.

MULTNOMAH BOOKS
www.mpbooks.com